SPOOKY SITES

RMS QUEEN MARY

THOMAS KINGSLEY TROUPE

A Shark Book
SEAHORSE PUBLISHING

Teaching Tips for Caregivers:

You can help your child learn by encouraging them to read widely, both as a leisure activity and as a way of satisfying their curiosity about the world. Reading helps build a strong foundation in language and literacy skills that will help your child succeed in school. This high-interest book will appeal to all readers in intermediate and middle school grades.

Use the following suggestions to help your child grow as a reader.

- Encourage them to read independently at home.
- Encourage them to practice reading aloud.
- Encourage activities that require reading.
- Establish a regular reading time.
- Have your child ask and answer questions about what they read.

Teaching Tips for Teachers:

Engage students throughout the reading process by asking questions like these.

Before Reading

- Ask, "What do you already know about this topic?"
- Ask, "What do you want to learn about this topic?"

During Reading

- Ask, "What is the author trying to teach you?"
- Ask, "How is this like something you have read or seen before?"
- Ask, "How do the text features (headings, index, etc.) help you understand the topic?"

After Reading

- Ask, "What interesting or fun fact did you learn?"
- Ask, "What questions do you still have about the topic? How could you find the answers?

TABLE OF CONTENTS

Haunts from the High Seas

You walk into the quiet, dark room. Your footsteps echo in the big, empty cruise ship. The air is heavy and cold, making you shiver. Your arms break out in goosebumps. You shine your flashlight around, looking for the exit. Maybe coming here alone wasn't the best idea.

Very faintly, you hear what sounds like children shouting. And is that a splashing sound? You stop and listen. Someone or something in the distance whistles. Your light reveals an old swimming pool. The pool is empty. Even so, you see a trail of wet footprints on the floor. Time to get off this boat!

The History of RMS *Queen Mary*

RMS *Queen Mary* was a British ocean liner that sailed across the Atlantic Ocean for 31 years. It was part of the Cunard-White Star Line, the company that owned the ill-fated *Titanic* decades earlier.

The construction of *Queen Mary* began in Scotland in 1930. But work on the mighty ship was paused during the Great Depression. It was finally ready for its **maiden voyage** on May 27, 1936. The ship sailed from Southampton, England, to New York City. With just one stop in France, the trip took about five days.

FRIGHTENING FACTS

The letters RMS stand for "Royal Mail Ship." Ships like this had a contract with the British government to carry mail along with passengers.

QUEEN MARY
LIVERPOOL

Queen Mary was large and powerful. It was 1,020 feet (311 meters) long and weighed more than 81,000 tons (73,000 metric tons).

The ship allowed 2,038 passengers to sail across the ocean in **luxury**. It had everything a traveler could want or need. *Queen Mary* had five lounges and dining areas, two cocktail bars, a beautiful ballroom, a squash court, and swimming pools. There was even a small hospital onboard for hurt or sick passengers.

FRIGHTENING FACTS

RMS *Queen Mary* is often compared to another famous ship, the *Titanic*. But *Titanic* sank on its maiden voyage in 1912. The bigger, faster *Queen Mary* made successful trips across the Atlantic Ocean for decades.

Birth of the Grey Ghost

After only three years of transporting the rich and famous, *Queen Mary* was given a new job. In 1939, it was drafted into the military to help transport **troops** during World War II. Britain was certain that the ship's speed and size would make it difficult for German U-boats to sink.

On its new voyages, as many as 15,000 soldiers were crammed onto the ship. To make more room, *Queen Mary* was stripped of its fancy interior. The ship's brightly colored smokestacks were painted gray. The portholes were welded shut. The once-beautiful ship earned a new nickname: The Grey Ghost.

Not everything went well for *Queen Mary* during the war. In 1942, the ship accidentally crashed into HMS *Curacoa*. The *Curacoa* was a smaller cruiser that was **escorting** *Queen Mary* along the Irish coastline. The bigger ship smashed into *Curacoa*, tearing it in half.

FRIGHTENING FACTS

Nazi leader Adolf Hitler offered 250,000 dollars to any submarine captain who could sink *Queen Mary*. It never happened!

Some crew members were killed instantly. Others drowned or died from **hypothermia** in the icy sea. *Queen Mary* could not stop to save them. That would have endangered the lives of thousands of soldiers on board. Sadly, more than 330 men lost their lives in the accident.

A New Afterlife?

After the war, *Queen Mary* was restored to her former glory. Beginning in 1947, the ship transported passengers across the Atlantic for the next two decades. On October 31, 1967, the ship took its final cruise, arriving in Long Beach, California. There, *Queen Mary* was converted into a floating hotel.

FRIGHTENING FACTS

Room B340 was combined with two other nearby rooms to make a larger hotel room. It didn't stop the hauntings.

People who have worked and stayed on the ocean liner hotel believe it's haunted. Maybe because of the ship's **storied** history, there are said to be around 150 spirits from the **afterlife** wandering its decks.

Room B340 is said to be the most haunted place on board. A passenger named Walter J. Adamson died there mysteriously in 1948. In that room, guests report covers ripped off the bed, phantom voices, and faucets that turn on and off by themselves.

PRESSURE
AHEAD STEAM
CONTROL PANEL
C
D
No 1Q
No 11
No 12

Real or Hoax?

Is RMS *Queen Mary* really haunted? Many believe it is, but **skeptics** are quick to claim that it's all just a **hoax.** Over the years, at least 47 people died on board. That doesn't include people killed during the HMS *Curacoa* tragedy. Believers point out that a place where so much death has occurred must have **paranormal** activity.

One famous death happened on July 10, 1966. John Pedder was an 18-year-old crewman who worked below deck. During a practice drill, Pedder tried to make his way through a self-closing, watertight door before it closed. He didn't make it. His body was crushed by the door. It is said that an **apparition** resembling Pedder has wandered around down there ever since.

FRIGHTENING FACTS

Swimming pools aboard *Queen Mary* have not been used for decades. But people have seen ghostly figures around the pools wearing 1930s-style swimwear. They've heard splashing and spotted wet footprints on the floor.

Paranormal Proof?

Many paranormal investigators are sure that *Queen Mary* is haunted. They've caught ghostly voices, or EVP (electronic voice phenomena), on their digital recorders. It's believed these voices could be from the dead who linger on the ship. When searching for spirits, investigators also use cameras to try and capture evidence of ghosts.

RMS *Queen Mary* is still open for business in Long Beach, California. Guests can stay in the fancy hotel rooms or just take a tour. There is even a Haunted Encounters Tour that explores all the spooky things that have happened on the ship. Maybe you'll run into something **supernatural** during your visit!

Be a Paranormal Investigator!

Whether it's really haunted or not, RMS *Queen Mary* is still a creepy place for the curious to explore. Are former crew members and passengers still moving between decks? Are blinking lights and creaking doors messages from the dead? No one knows for sure. But one thing is certain: The legendary history of the big ship is full of frights

Do you want to be a paranormal investigator? You can! All you really need is a flashlight, an audio recorder, and some bravery. Go to a dark, creepy place. Look around and ask questions. Record the whole EVP session. When you play the recording back, you might hear strange things. Is it something paranormal trying to talk to you? It could be!

Glossary

afterlife (AF-tur-life): an existence after the death of a person's physical body

apparition (ap-puh-RI-shuhn): a supernatural appearance of a person or thing; a ghost or specter

escorting (ES-kort-ing): traveling beside someone or something else to provide protection

hoax (hohks): a trick that makes people believe something that is not true

hypothermia (hye-puh-THUR-mee-uh): a dangerous or fatal condition in which a person's body temperature drops very low

luxury (LUHK-shur-ee): having things that are pleasant, beautiful, or expensive, but not necessary

maiden voyage (MAY-duhn VOI-ij): the first trip taken by a particular ship

paranormal (pair-uh-NOR-muhl): something that cannot be explained by science

skeptics (SKEP-tiks): people who have doubts or questions about whether something is true

storied (STOR-eed): having an interesting or unusual history

supernatural (soo-pur-NACH-ur-uhl): existing outside of human experience or knowledge

troops (troops): soldiers organized into groups

Index

After Reading Questions

1. Why do you think *Queen Mary* was retired as a passenger ship?

2. Why might ghosts live on *Queen Mary*? Whose ghosts might they be?

3. Give reasons why someone might choose to stay or not stay in Room B340 on *Queen Mary*.

4. Explain how *Queen Mary* got the nickname "The Grey Ghost."

About the Author

Thomas Kingsley Troupe is the author of over 200 books for young readers. When he's not writing, he enjoys reading, playing video games, and investigating haunted places with the Twin Cities Paranormal Society. Otherwise, he's probably taking a nap or something. Thomas lives in Woodbury, Minnesota, with his two sons.

Written by: Thomas Kingsley Troupe
Design by: Under the Oaks Media
Editor: Kim Thompson

Photo credits: Keystone Press / Alamy Stock Photo: p. 7; Chronicle / Alamy Stock Photo: p. 8; Smith Archive / Alamy Stock Photo: p. 9; SuperStock / Alamy Stock Photo: p. 10, 10-11; All other images from Shuterstock or in the public domain.

Library of Congress PCN Data
RMS *Queen Mary* / Thomas Kingsley Troupe
Spooky Sites
ISBN 979-8-8904-2689-5 (hard cover)
ISBN 979-8-8904-2717-5 (paperback)
ISBN 979-8-8904-2745-8 (EPUB)
ISBN 979-8-8904-2773-1 (eBook)
Library of Congress Control Number: 2023923672

Printed in the United States of America.

Seahorse Publishing Company
seahorsepub.com

Published in the United States
Seahorse Publishing
PO Box 771325
Coral Springs, FL 33077

SEAHORSE PUBLISHING